SHIRE NATURAL I

CW00959171

POPLARᴕ
of the British Isles

THERESA BRENDELL

CONTENTS

Cover: *The male catkins of black poplar (Populus nigra) shed their scales before the crimson anthers release pollen.*

Series editor: Jim Flegg.

Copyright © 1990 by Theresa Brendell. First published 1990.
Number 58 in the Shire Natural History series. ISBN 0 7478 0093 6.

British Library Cataloguing in Publication Data:
Brendell, Theresa.
Poplars of the British Isles.
1. Great Britain. Poplars.
I. Title.
583.981

Printed in Great Britain by C. I. Thomas & Sons (Haverfordwest) Ltd, Press Buildings, Merlins Bridge, Haverfordwest, Dyfed SA61 1XF.

Introduction

Poplars and aspens are trees with light open crowns and often fluttering foliage. They are found mostly in the northern hemisphere, scattered but common in suitable habitats in regions with a temperate climate; the greatest numbers of species are found in eastern Asia and eastern North America. Poplars are related to willows and sallows and are grouped with them in the Salicaceae family. Though it is easy to differentiate between a willow and a poplar, they do share certain biological characteristics, not least of which is a tendency to produce hybrids. It is generally agreed that there are between thirty and forty species worldwide, all belonging to the genus *Populus*.

Poplar trees are fast-growing pioneers that can take root on damp unstabilised soils or amongst boulders and screes, in moist open situations with unimpeded light. They occur naturally in open valley bottoms or on hillsides, rather than in forests or dense woodland. Like many other trees, their natural distribution has been extended and their boundaries have been obscured by man's interference. Poplars of many kinds are now seen to flourish in places where they would not become established spontaneously.

From fossil evidence, it can be seen that aspens at least have grown over some parts of Britain since the late-glacial stage of the last ice age, about eleven thousand to twelve thousand years ago. Aspen pollen grains and other fossil fragments of this age have been recorded from deposits in Ireland, north-west England and south Scotland. Certainly by the bronze age both aspen pollen and charcoal have been identified from sites throughout England, Ireland and Scotland.

Although there are only two species native to Britain, black poplar (*Populus nigra*) and aspen (*P. tremula*), other poplar species feature prominently on the moist fertile soils of central and southern England and also flourish in lowland Ireland, Wales and Scotland. Only aspen tolerates upland conditions. The non-natives include white poplar (*P. alba*), a well established introduction from Europe, and grey poplar (*P.* x *canescens*), which is a hybrid between white poplar and aspen, also originating from Europe. Extensively planted are the many similar hybrids which may be grouped together under the heading of Euramerican or black hybrid poplars (*P.* x *canadensis* vars.). Resulting from a cross between the European black poplar and the North American cottonwood (*P. deltoides*), numerous cultivars have been selectively bred for their wood, and they can be difficult to identify.

Other exotic species, such as the balsam poplars, are seen chiefly in parks, gardens and arboreta, whilst in both town and country the Lombardy poplar (*P. nigra* var. *italica*) is planted for its distinctive appearance and as a shelter tree.

The genus *Populus* is subdivided into five sections: *Populus,* the white poplars and aspens; *Aegiros,* the black poplars and black (Euramerican) hybrids; *Tacamahaca,* the balsam poplars; *Leucoides,* a group of rather obscure species mostly restricted to the Far East; and *Turanga,* which comprises only one species, the Euphrates poplar. Except for the Chinese necklace poplar (*P. lasiocarpa*), species in sections *Leucoides* and *Turanga* are not known in Britain. The Chinese necklace poplar is a decorative tree with very large leaves and is occasionally planted in parks and gardens. Because of this poor representation, sections *Leucoides* and *Turanga* are not covered here. The poplars discussed in this book include all those species and hybrids likely to be encountered in Britain, whether growing wild or planted in gardens, in places of amenity or in plantations.

Description

In their native ranges poplars are tall trees often exceeding 30 metres (100 feet), but Britain is not the natural home of most species and they do not attain their full height there. Aspen and white poplar may reach about 20 metres (66 feet), and even 26 metres (85 feet) has been recorded for a white poplar in

2

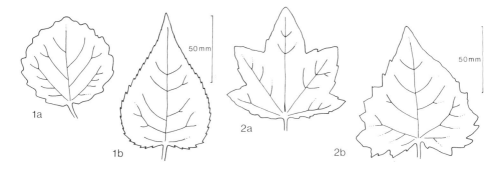

1. *Aspen (Populus tremula). The leaves are almost circular in outline (a), except for those borne on young sucker shoots (b), which are heart-shaped.*

2. *Leaf-shape in white poplar (Populus alba): (a) a leaf from a sucker shoot or tip of a long fast-growing shoot; (b) a leaf from a short slow-growing shoot.*

Oxford, but both species are usually much smaller trees or untidy bushes. The grey poplar is more vigorous, sometimes reaching 30-5 metres (100-15 feet), and the black Italian poplar (Euramerican hybrid *P. x canadensis* var. *serotina*) may surpass 40 metres (130 feet).

The symmetrical flame- or cone-shaped appearance of the young poplar changes as the tree matures, eventually making a large open crown. Many mature poplars have an irregular branching pattern. Black poplar develops a broad heavy crown with arching branches, the lower boughs arising from a fairly short trunk. A mature black Italian poplar is an untidy tree, the uneven growth of branches making it lop-sided. An aspen grove has an airy appearance, the trees retaining their lightly branched crowns even when mature. Grey and white poplars are more graceful and billowing, often leaning, and their lowest branches intermingle with a thicket of suckers. In contrast, the acutely upswept branches and twigs of the Lombardy poplar produce the familiar plume-shaped, or fastigiate, tree. These branches start low down on the trunk within 1 metre (3 feet) of the ground. The Euramerican hybrid *P. x robusta* has a narrow crown borne on a tall branchless trunk, which makes it useful commercially.

The bark of most poplars becomes grey and fissured with age, at least on the lower portion of the mature trunk, but the upper part and larger branches are usually smoother and paler. White poplar has gleaming white bark on the upper trunk. Although it is often said that the bark of grey poplar is pale grey, in fact it varies from a light greenish olive to white. Both these poplars bear conspicuous rows of black diamond-shaped lenticels (pores). In contrast, the black poplar owes its English name to the uniformly dark colour of its bark. A further distinguishing feature of this species is the development of large rough patches known as burrs that protrude from the bole to give a lumpy outline, a characteristic not inherited by hybrid offspring. Aspen and the western balsam poplar (*P. trichocarpa*) have an olive-green bark.

Though they are considered by foresters to be fairly wind-firm, the tendency of maturing poplar trees to bear large uneven branches makes them susceptible to strong winds, as seen in the violent storm of 16th October 1987, which wrought havoc throughout southern England. Young trees and Lombardy poplars fared reasonably well, but older trees lost heavy boughs or were completely uprooted. Without such disasters black poplars may live for three hundred years, developing a buttressed trunk. White poplars can be similarly long-lived, but aspens and Lombardies have a relatively shorter life, rarely reaching one hundred years.

Poplars are all deciduous, with simple alternate leaves. Their leaves are broad, ranging in shape from the nearly round leaves of aspens to the triangular leaves of some Euramerican hybrids and the almost palmate leaves of white poplar. There are two kinds of shoots, slower-growing lateral spurs and fast-growing leading shoots, including sucker shoots when present. Aspen, white and grey poplars exhibit considerable variation in the size and shape of the leaves borne by these shoots. Aspen foliage is least confusing — most of the leaves are typically rounded, with wavy edges and shallow teeth, and it is only on the suckers that pointed heart-shaped leaves appear. Leaves on the slow-growing shoots of white poplars are more or less egg-shaped in outline, sparsely toothed, with shallow uneven lobes. Leaves on the leading shoots are distinctly and more regularly lobed and very similar in shape to a small sycamore leaf. The lower surface of these palmate leaves and the tips of the shoots are thickly covered with snowy white hairs, giving them a cotton-wool appearance.

Leaves of grey poplar are intermediate in shape and hairiness between aspen and white poplar, with considerable variation in the characteristics of leaves on slow- and fast-growing shoots. As well as the range of leaf-types on each individual grey poplar, different trees exhibit a graduated series of intermediates more closely resembling aspen leaves at one extreme and white poplar at the other. The triangular or lozenge-shaped leaves of black and hybrid black poplars are more uniform. They have a whitish waxy margin and are all evenly and bluntly serrate, or toothed. It can be difficult to separate black poplar leaves from those of the hybrids by shape alone, but only the hybrid leaves have a pair of small knobbly glands where the leaf-stalk joins the blade. Balsam poplar leaves are bluntly toothed but lack the translucent margin. These and the black poplars have hairless leaves, although the young shoots of black poplar are downy.

Many poplars have petioles (leaf-stalks) that are flattened laterally. The petioles are also relatively long, which causes the leaves to flutter in the wind. This is most noticeable in the aspen, where the leaves tremble in the slightest breeze, giving rise to the belief in folklore that the Cross was made from aspen

3. *Variation in leaf-shape of grey poplar (Populus x canescens). Leaves on the slow-growing shoots tend to be rounded in outline (a), similar to aspen leaves. Fast-growing and sucker shoots bear large toothed leaves (f), but intermediates in size and shape (b, c, d and e) abound.*

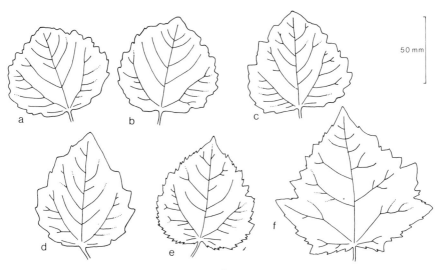

4. *Black poplar (Populus nigra). This mature tree shows the heavy arching boughs typical of this species.*

wood and that the aspen is still quivering with shame.

In winter, the buds are protected by overlapping scales. Buds of balsam and black poplars are sticky, and those of the former are extremely strongly scented. As the leaves unfurl in spring, their heavy scent pervades the air for quite some distance. These trees are often planted in gardens for this reason, but whilst some people find the smell very pleasant others find it cloying and sickly.

Prolific sucker growth is characteristic of many poplars, including the aspen, the white and grey poplars and the balsams. Suckers are adventitious shoots that arise from tree roots, sometimes at quite a distance from the main trunk. Suckers may be the only natural means by which some poplars propagate in the wild, and it is vegetative reproduction by suckers which causes the thickets along stream-

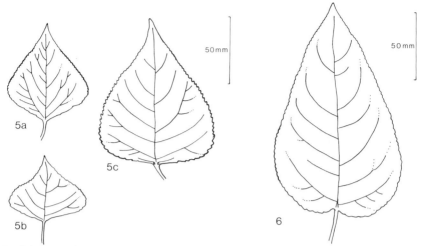

5. *Leaf-shape in black poplars and the hybrid black poplars is fairly constant; (a) black poplar (Populus nigra); (b) Lombardy poplar (P. nigra var. italica); and (c) a hybrid black poplar (P. x canadensis var. serotina), the lower surface showing the two small glands at the base of the leaf-blade.*

6. *Western balsam poplar (Populus trichocarpa). There is less variation in shape within this and other species of balsam poplar, but there is a wide size range.*

sides, lakes and broads. Poplar scrub is seldom desirable in parks and gardens and those most prone to sucker growth, notably the balsam poplar (*P. x candicans*), are best avoided. Black poplar and the Euramerican hybrids do not produce suckers.

Like willows and sallows, poplar trees are single-sexed, bearing either male or female catkins. Unlike the mostly upright, insect-pollinated catkins of willows, however, those of poplars are pendulous and exclusively wind-pollinated. Catkins are borne on short stalks and open in February and March, well before the leaves appear. Trees of both sexes seldom occur in hybrid poplars. Grey poplars are predominantly male, although female trees are known. The Euramerican hybrids *P. x canadensis* vars. *eugenei* and *serotina*, and *P. x robusta* are exclusively male trees, and *P. x canadensis* vars. *marilandica* and *regenerata* are female trees. Male trees of white poplar, though common in more southerly parts of Europe, do not seem to thrive in Britain and are very rare there.

Poplar catkins consist of numerous small flowers, each with a bract or catkin scale. In both sexes, the perianth (petals and sepals) has been reduced to a thin flattish or cup-like disc. The flowers are closely packed on the male catkin and are much more loosely spaced on the female. These wind-pollinated flowers have no bright petals or sweetly scented nectar to attract insect pollinators. Instead, the sexual parts of the flowers are clearly exposed, so that the pollen may readily be wafted from the anthers of the male flowers to the stigmas of the female. The conspicuous anthers of most poplars are a deep red and when ripe they release copious amounts of powdery pollen. The number of stamens, even within a species, varies: white poplar has five to ten, and black Italian poplar has ten to twenty-five. Despite the lack of petals, mature male catkins can be very showy, especially those of poplars in the section *Populus* (white, grey and aspen), whose densely clustered flowers have pale-haired scales and purplish red anthers. Female flowers have a globular to narrowly pear-shaped ovary with two greenish, lobed stigmas.

6

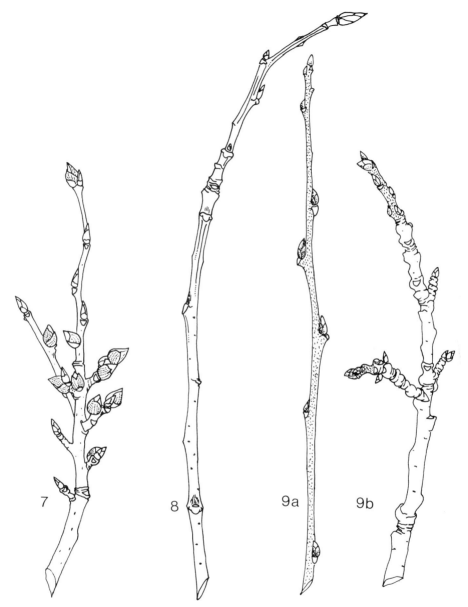

7. *An aspen twig in winter, showing fat catkin buds and smaller, narrower leaf buds.*

8. *A winter twig of hybrid black poplar. They are smooth and angular.*

9. *Winter twigs of grey poplar: (a) the tip of last season's fast-growing shoot; (b) a slow-growing twig. The last season's growth still retains a thin coat of hairs. Notice the straight smooth appearance of (a), whereas (b) is knobbly with short side spurs.*

10. *White poplars (Populus alba). The outlines of their light open crowns are obscured by the vigorous undergrowth of suckers.*

11 (left). *Grey poplar (Populus x canescens). This once splendid tree was battered by a storm but is now making strong new growth.*
12 (right). *Lombardy poplars (Populus nigra var. italica). The bright green foliage turns yellow in autumn.*

13 (left). *Grey poplar (Populus x canescens). The white hairs on the lower leaf surface are not usually persistent.*

14 (right). *Black poplar (Populus nigra), showing the bright breen shiny triangular leaves.*

15. *Aspen (Populus tremula) foliage in midsummer. Notice the long petioles (leaf stalks).*

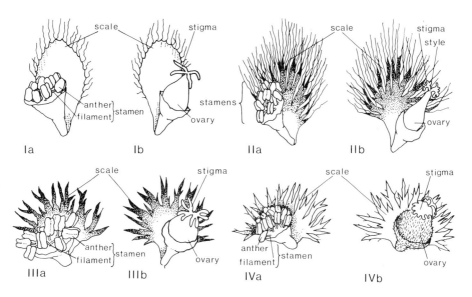

16. *(I) White poplar (Populus alba) flowers: (a) male, (b) female. (II) Aspen (Populus tremula) flowers: (a) male, (b) female. (III) Black poplar (Populus nigra) flowers: (a) male, (b) female. (IV) Western balsam poplar (Populus trichocarpa) flowers: (a) male, (b) female.*

The catkin scales are typically deeply divided, with the exception of those of white poplar. Only scales of white, grey and aspen poplars have long hairs; those of black poplar and the black hybrid poplars are very finely divided but not hairy, and those of the balsam poplars sometimes bear short hairs. Male catkins fall when they have shed their pollen. Female catkins shed their scales and lengthen, so that the green developing fruits appear to resemble a strand of beads. Some of these catkins become quite long, for instance those of the Chinese necklace poplar are 20 cm (8 inches) and those of the balsam poplar (*P. balsamifera*) are 20-30 cm (8-12 inches).

The two-valved fruit capsules ripen in late spring or early summer. They split in warm dry weather, releasing numerous very tiny seeds embedded in tightly packed white cotton floss. This soon fluffs up so that prodigious quantities are dispersed by the slightest breeze. Even unfertilised seedless ovules produce this floss, and the amount released from a group or row of female trees may well be

a considerable nuisance, especially near houses or along pavements, upon which it may collect in drifts.

Spread far and wide by the wind, the seeds contain very little food reserves and so remain viable for only a few days. Within this short period, they need to alight on bare damp soil for successful germination to ensue.

IDENTIFICATION OF POPLARS

With relatively few species of poplars seen in Britain, identification should be easy. However, the presence of both natural and man-made hybrids makes it difficult to identify some trees, especially grey and white poplars and hybrid black poplars.

Grey poplar is a variable hybrid with some individuals very close to white poplar in appearance. These trees have often been wrongly identified as white poplar, especially when the judgement has been based on the characteristics of foliage and bark alone. It is therefore important to know the sex of a tree, as the presence of male catkins would almost always indicate a grey poplar, and female catkins would confirm a white poplar. Grey poplar is less likely to be confused with aspen, even though it is possible that back-crossing with *P. tremula* may occur occasionally.

Far more difficult is the identification of the Euramerican hybrid poplars. This large group comprises a complex series of hybrids between the European black poplar (*P. nigra*) and its varieties and the North American cottonwood (*P. deltoides*) and its varieties. The cottonwood was probably introduced to Europe in the eighteenth century, after which spontaneous hybrids soon appeared. They were clearly very vigorous trees and therefore soon began to attract the attention of foresters. The number of artificially bred hybrids quickly rose.

Eventually a more systematic approach

subgenus → species ↓ character	Populus · alba	Populus · tremula	Populus · x canescens	Aegiros · nigra	Aegiros · nigra var. italica	Aegiros · x canadensis	Aegiros · x robusta	Tacamahaca · balsamifera	Tacamahaca · trichocarpa	Tacamahaca · x candicans	Leucoides · lasiocarpa
Crown broad, spreading	●	●	●	●		●		○	●	●	○
Crown narrow, upright					●	○	●				
Buds sticky		●		●	●	●	●	●	●	●	○
Leaf-shape triangular					●	●	●				
Leaf-shape diamond				●		○					
Leaf-shape heart		○								●	●
Leaf-shape round		●	●								
Leaf-shape ovate	○		●					●	●		
Leaf-shape lobed	●		○								
Margin entire								○			
Margin toothed	○	●	●	●	●	●	●		○	●	●
Margin wavy	○		●								
Upper leaf surface dark green	●	●	●				●	●	●	●	
Upper leaf surface pale or bright				●	●	●				◉	
Lower surface hairy	●		●	○					○	○	●
Pair of glands at base of blade						●	●				
Petiole flattened sideways	○	●	●	●	●	●	●				
Male trees only			●		●	○	●				
Female trees only	●					○				●	
Both sexes known	●	●		●				●	●		●

Column notes:
- x canescens: Only female trees in UK; very white shoots and bark
- tremula: Foliage very fluttery
- x canescens: Often a large tree
- nigra: Trunk heavily and conspicuously 'bossed'
- nigra var. italica: Narrow plume-shaped crown
- x canadensis: All hybrids single-sexed — some male, some female
- balsamifera: Bark has pinkish fissures, young shoots round
- trichocarpa: An aromatic, graceful tree, young shoots angled
- x candicans: Sucker growth very prolific
- lasiocarpa: Huge leaves, with red veins and petioles

● Character present

○ Character either present sometimes or present to a certain extent

17. *Identification guide to native species of Populus, and those introductions and hybrids most likely to be encountered.*

11

18 (left). *Grey poplar (Populus x canescens). This photograph shows clearly the scales and stamens of the male catkin.*

19 (right). *Aspen (Populus tremula). These are female catkins, the tiny hairy scales can just be seen falling away from the pear-shaped oviaries.*

20 (left). *A female clone of hybrid black poplar (Populus x canadensis var.). The ripe capsule splits to release tiny seeds embedded in cottony threads, which quickly become fluffy.*

21 (right). *Black poplar (Populus nigra): female catkins showing lobed stigmas.*

22. *Aspen (Populus tremula) catkins appear well before the leaves. These are male. Their fluffy appearance is due to many hairy scales.*

23. *White poplar (Populus alba): female catkins, the stem covered with white hairs.*

to poplar breeding was instigated, largely as a result of a conference held in Paris in 1947, shortly after which the International Poplar Commission was established. In Britain poplars incurred Forestry Commission interest, chiefly because of their very rapid growth and good yields. Fast-grown timber is always of value, and the merits of the black hybrids far surpass those of either parent. Black poplar, even in optimum parts of its range, is a relatively slow-growing tree, its thick trunk burry and useless for commercial purposes, and the cottonwood does not grow well in the British Isles. In contrast their hybrids have tall trunks free from burrs and are much better suited to the British climate, growing faster there than any other tree.

All the hybrids are easily propagated by cuttings, to give clones of genetically identical trees. A very large number of clones has now been bred and put on trial. Many of these clones are closely alike in appearance, differing only in disease resistance, timber quality or growth rates. Hybrids between black and balsam poplars have also been bred.

The table (figure 17) is a guide to the identification of all the species and hybrids most likely to be encountered in Britain.

Distribution and ecology

Estimates of the numbers and distribution of white, grey and black poplars in Britain have frequently been inaccurate. Confusion between white and grey poplars has existed since they were first distinguished in the late sixteenth century, with many botanists up to the 1960s believing grey poplar to be a native species. It is now known to be a hybrid, and a well established introduction. Furthermore, hybrid Euramerican poplars are sometimes wrongly identified as the true native black poplar, overestimating the abundance of this now rare tree.

ASPEN, *Populus tremula*

The aspen is widespread and common throughout Britain and Ireland, and it is the only poplar to be found in upland areas. However, although it is a hardy tree, tolerant of a wide range of environmental conditions, aspen does not grow as well in Britain as it does in Poland, Russia and Scandinavia, where it is an important timber tree.

In southern England aspens grow beside rivers and lakes, as patches of scrub on heathlands, and as a component of broad-leaved woodlands, especially along the margins and in wet boggy places. In northern England, Wales, Scotland and Ireland aspens are an increasingly prominent part of the vegetation, as they freely colonise stream and loch sides and mountain slopes. Even in the north, aspens in sheltered valleys will grow into well shaped trees 12 metres (40 feet) tall, but besides lochs on wind-swept rocky shores, they remain as small gnarled bushes.

WHITE POPLAR, *Populus alba*

Most white poplars in Britain and Ireland have been planted either because of the attractive appearance of the young shoots or to bind the loose soils of river, stream and canal banks. They are well established locally only in the south-east and East Anglia, although even here natural regeneration is by means of suckers, as British white poplars are all female. White poplar seldom grows as an isolated tree if left to develop naturally, as suckers spring up around it, making a dense scrub. These bushy thickets are a characteristic feature of the vegetation beside watercourses and near the sea in the south and east.

GREY POPLAR, *Populus x canescens*

Possibly the first grey poplars were brought to the British Isles from Holland in the early seventeenth century, although it is also feasible that aspens and white poplars growing in proximity in England have occasionally hybridised. Many grey poplars have been planted, and they are now naturalised in many areas. They are much more widespread and far outnumber white poplars in Britain and Ireland. They regenerate freely from suckers, making an impenetrable thicket alongside rivers, streams and ditches, and in damp hollows. Most abundant in the south-east, the grey poplar nevertheless thrives in suitable niches in Wales, northern England and well into Scotland, where it is often found in disturbed habitats near roads, towns and wasteland as far north as Argyll and Forfar. Like its parents, it is fairly salt-tolerant and will also flourish near the coast.

The mis-identification of grey poplar for white has led in the past to an overestimate of the number and distribution of the white poplar, which in many places is entirely absent except as a planted ornamental tree. White poplars are native to the countries of southern Europe, western Asia and north Africa, all regions with much warmer summers than those experienced in Britain. Because of its less exacting requirements, the grey poplar is able to do better in cooler climates and on poorer soils.

BLACK POPLAR, *Populus nigra*

The black poplar is indigenous to much of southern and central Europe and western Asia. The black poplars of Britain are a remnant population of this variable species, surviving at the north-west limit of its range. The British trees are considered to be a distinct variety, var. *betulifolia,* that also occurs in France and parts of Germany. It is distinguished solely by the fleeting presence of fine hairs on the young shoots, leaf veins and petioles. Black poplar was once a distinctive feature of lowland river valleys throughout much of southern England. Deliberate planting has concealed its natural boundaries, but it is thought native to the area south of a line from the Mersey to the Humber estuaries, excluding most of Wales, Cornwall and parts of Devon.

Though previously so typical of river and stream sides and damp woodlands, this poplar is now one of Britain's rarest native trees. Often confused with Euramerican hybrid black poplars, its sorry plight remained undetected until the 1970s and 1980s. Surveys then revealed that its distribution is sparse and that the thinly scattered trees do not appear to be regenerating naturally. The reasons for this are probably twofold.

In times when the land was less affected by drainage schemes and waterways management, rivers and streams swollen by storms more frequently burst their banks, depositing silt and debris on the surrounding water meadows and carving out new areas of bare soil, exposed and ready to receive seeds when the waters subsided. These flood plains are prime sites for agriculture and, now drained and farmed, no longer provide the suitably moist fertile bare ground for the successful germination and growth of black poplar seeds.

Secondly, as well as a reduction in suitable sites for seedling establishment, the numbers of seeds themselves has fallen. Although once commonly planted in farmyards, cuttings from male trees were chosen, as the masses of fluffy seeds were a nuisance near the farmhouse and buildings. This has gradually contributed to an imbalance in the ratio of male to female trees. The number of females has dwindled to such an extent that there are now thought to be only three places where the two sexes are close enough for pollination — and hence seed production — to occur.

As the industrial revolution gathered momentum in the nineteenth century and smoky cities expanded, the black poplar was found to be surprisingly pollution-tolerant, flourishing well in urban conditions. It was planted extensively, particularly in the Midlands, where a local strain became known as the Manchester poplar. It has also been planted sporadically north and west of its natural range in Britain. In ideal conditions of deep fertile moist soil it grows tall, developing the typical spreading profile that was once so familiar. It can tolerate much poorer conditions on meagre soils, although its growth will be stunted.

The Lombardy poplar is an introduced variety of black poplar. Originating, as its name suggests, in north Italy, it was brought to Britain in the mid-eighteenth century. Only male Lombardy poplars are known, and female trees of similar shape are most likely hybrids or another variety of black poplar. The narrow plume-like shape of this tree, with its

24. *Balsam poplar (Populus balsamifera). A grove of straight saplings, from suckers, surrounds the parent tree.*

25 (below left). *The storm of October 1987 demolished the grey poplars growing by this roadside near the river Wey in Farnham, Surrey. The following spring a carpet of suckers sprang up from the still living roots.*

26 (below right). *Aspen (Populus tremula) trees at the edge of woodland, with young suckers encroaching on the buttercups.*

27. *White poplar (Populus alba). This photograph shows the frosty white appearance of the young shoots and foliage.*

upswept, almost erect branches, make it one of the easiest trees to identify. It is frequently planted in flat lowland parts of Britain, as an amenity tree in parks, arboreta and (less suitably) gardens in town and country, and for screening and shelter in both urban and rural environments. When planted in tight rows, the Lombardy poplar grows quickly to conceal buildings and industrial sites. Growing best in the Midlands and southern England, it nevertheless is a hardy tree frequently planted in Scotland.

COTTONWOOD, *Populus deltoides*

Cottonwood is included because it is one of the parents of the hybrid black poplars. In its pure form this North American species is not well suited to the British climate. Consequently it is an uncommon poplar, planted occasionally in arboreta, where individuals may reach a height of 27 metres (90 feet).

EURAMERICAN HYBRID POPLARS

This large group is the mainstay of poplar cultivation in the United Kingdom. As they are dependent on a combination of hot summers and a moist soil

in order to maintain the high growth rates required, it is only in the southern half of England where they can be satisfactorily grown for commercial purposes. However, these trees are hardy and will flourish as far north as Inverness in Scotland, but with a much slower rate of growth. When travelling across the countryside, by rail or road, it is evident that hybrid black poplars abound. They have been planted in odd pockets and inaccessible corners of agricultural land, alongside fields and ditches, beside railways and industrial complexes. Many of these are young trees, less than forty years old. Their light open canopy allows smaller shrubs and wild flowers to grow beneath them.

It is not possible to comment on all of the very numerous hybrids and cultivars. Only a few of the older and better known hybrids have been selected for inclusion in this book.

BLACK ITALIAN POPLAR, *Populus* x *canadensis* var. *serotina*

One of the first hybrid blacks to gain popularity in Britain and therefore one of the few old enough to display a fully

17

mature crown, this poplar is asymmetrical and heavily branched. It is a hardy tree.

Populus x canadensis var. marilandica

This spreading tree has been planted less often than the black Italian poplar, chiefly because they are all female trees shedding a large amount of floss in midsummer.

RAILWAY POPLAR, Populus x canadensis var. regenerata

This almost sterile female hybrid is unusual in that it produces very little fluff. It was considered to be a good plantation tree, but its susceptibility to bacterial canker has been a great disadvantage. It gained its common name because so many have been planted near railway stations, sidings and goods yards.

Populus x robusta

Favoured by commercial growers, this rather narrow-crowned hybrid grows very rapidly. It is most likely to be seen in poplar plantations in southern England. It was first seen in France in 1895.

WESTERN BALSAM POPLAR, Populus trichocarpa

One of the largest poplars when in its native homelands of the western seaboard of North America, this species is probably now the most commonly planted balsam poplar in Britain. It grows especially well in the wetter regions of the west, in England, Wales, Scotland and Ireland, but its susceptibility to bacterial canker limits any commercial use. It is a popular tree for parks and gardens and is planted on grassy banks by roadsides. Western balsams growing in Britain are probably all male trees. Though they are propagated from suckers, sucker growth is not as vigorous as in the other balsam poplars hardy in Britain.

BALSAM POPLAR OR TACAMAHAC, Populus balsamifera

This smaller tree originates from eastern North America and is less well known in Britain. It is occasionally planted by roadsides and in gardens and not infrequently seen in tree collections in botanical gardens. A cross between this poplar

and the western balsam poplar resulted in a fast-growing clone known as TT32, but hopes that it would prove resistant to bacterial canker proved unfounded.

BALSAM POPLAR, Populus x candicans

The ancestry of this poplar is unclear, though it is most likely to be a cross between P. balsamifera and P. deltoides. It was introduced to Britain from North America in the eighteenth century. Its present-day distribution reflects the extent to which it has been planted in the past, as a growth of bushy suckers often persists in hedgerows, neglected areas and unkempt gardens. It is still occasionally planted as a fast-growing hedge or border around farms or gardens but it cannot be considered ideal — the suckers sprout most abundantly, pushing up through pavements, around sheds and garages, quickly producing masses of large-leaved sticky shoots. It is a female hybrid, but apparently sterile.

Like the western balsam poplar and tacamahac, this hybrid also grows well in Scotland. Balsam poplars thus feature prominently in the tree-planting programmes that have been undertaken in and around large cities such as Glasgow, where local councils have been improving the urban environment.

CHINESE NECKLACE POPLAR, Populus lasiocarpa

From central China, this tree is likely to be found only in arboreta, parks and gardens in south and south-west England.

OTHER POPLAR HYBRIDS

Hybrids between P. nigra and P. trichocarpa have also been bred specially for the commercial market. Trials of a number of clones have shown that although they are very vigorous they are unfortunately prone to bacterial canker.

ECOLOGY

Poplars are pioneer plants, so called because by virtue of their light windborne seeds they are able to colonise disturbed, often unconsolidated ground quickly. Many pioneer species are small annuals, for example weeds of gardens and arable land. All pioneer plants have seeds that can germinate quickly and produce fast-growing shoots. Provided their seeds alight on moist soils, poplars and the related willows germinate immediately on landing in summer. Tiny seedlings develop within six days. However, the necessity for soil moisture restricts successful germination to damp places: silts freshly deposited after flooding, landslips of river or stream banks, and beside newly dug ditches or canals. In Britain only two species are able to spread by seed in this way, black poplar and aspen, but poplars that spread by means of suckers are also restricted to similar habitats. Sucker-producing poplars play a most important part in the stabilisation of riverbanks.

Seedlings that germinate on bare ground can grow very fast, enabling young poplars to compete successfully against slower-growing rivals. Seedlings are not likely to survive in dense woodland or amongst tall herbaceous vegetation. Typical habitats for poplars to become established include wet woodland margins and open banks beside watercourses. Environments that have been disturbed by man and new habitats that have been created by road building, flooding old gravel pits or digging drainage ditches also provide the moist open conditions ideal for poplars.

As well as the need for light, poplars require an abundant water supply but, unlike willows and sallows, they cannot tolerate a waterlogged or anaerobic soil. Poplar roots extend and ramify at the water table, where both soil and soil water are adequately oxygenated. Poplars cultivated commercially will not maintain a good rate of growth unless sufficient water is available.

However, in order to achieve their full potential height, poplars also require warmth. Except for aspen, most of the poplars found in Britain have a northern hemisphere distribution centred on southern Europe, western Asia and North America, in regions with a reliably long hot summer. In particular, Britain is at the very edge of the natural range of black poplar and just beyond that of white poplar, so both these species seldom attain their full dimensions there.

Aspens will proliferate readily in low-land habitats but are not confined to low altitudes. They are less dependent on the high water content of the soil than other poplars but they are very intolerant of shading. It is this need for plenty of light that restricts aspens to open situations, heathlands and woodland clearings and margins in the south and east, and open, often very exposed, valleys and mountain slopes in the north and west. Aspens are found in gullies at altitudes of 500 metres (1650 feet) in northern England.

On exposed mountainsides, often in wet flushes prone to soil erosion, stunted aspen bushes frequently grow together with similarly low-growing bushes of tea-leaved willow (*Salix phylicifolia*). At lower altitudes on the more level areas of the north and west, aspens and hazel (*Corylus avellana*) are often co-dominant in hedges and copses. Aspen, white and grey poplar are also tolerant of salt winds and sea spray and therefore may be seen as wind-swept thickets in some coastal regions.

Poplars in general are best suited to neutral soils, although they are lime-tolerant provided that there is an adequate water supply. Most kinds will not grow well on acid peat, but balsam poplars and aspen have a greater tolerance of acid conditions than other poplars, aspens in particular growing on sandy or peaty soils.

Thus it becomes apparent that the environmental conditions of light, moisture and warmth limit the distribution of both native species and the successful growth of introduced poplars in Britain.

Growth and propagation

The tiny seeds of poplars have a very limited viability and, once shed, they stay alive for only a few days. In order to germinate, they need damp bare soil. Because they are viable for such a short time they cannot be stored, so most poplars for amenity and commercial purposes are propagated from suckers or cuttings. Hybrids occurring only as males

19

(*P.* x *canadensis* var. *serotina*) or females (*P.* x *canadensis* var. *regenerata*) obviously cannot be propagated by seed, and these are also multiplied by cuttings.

Poplars grow quickly, some cultivars especially so, but as a warm summer and a constant and adequate supply of water are necessary for optimum rates of growth, most poplar cultivation is limited to the rich lowland loams of the southern half of England. Though late to open their leaves, poplars have a long growing season from June to mid September.

Propagating poplars by vegetative means, whether from cuttings or suckers, is easy and has advantages for the commercial grower. Chief amongst them is the possibility of establishing whole plantations of a single clone — genetically identical trees. This is very useful when uniformity of characteristics such as timber quality and disease resistance are paramount.

Not all species will root readily from cuttings. For instance, the aspen is particularly difficult to propagate in this way, but it can regenerate naturally from seed and will also spread by means of suckers. Similarly, it may be difficult to root cuttings of white poplar, so, as no white poplar seed is produced in Britain, natural regeneration and deliberate propagation are both entirely from suckers. Grey poplar is also propagated from suckers. All balsam poplars, both the true species such as western balsam and the hybrid balsams, can be grown from cuttings very easily. The native black poplar can spread by seed but is usually grown from cuttings. Fortunately for the forester, all the Euramerican hybrid poplars are easily reproduced from cuttings, which grow well after rooting.

Cuttings are taken from one-year-old shoots, usually in early winter after the wood has ripened. About 23 cm (9 inches) long, they are pushed vertically into well prepared soil so that the top of the cutting is level with the soil surface. These root readily and grow quickly, so that in the first year they reach 1.5 to 2.5 metres (5 to 8 feet). At the end of this growing season the new shoots are cut back close to the ground, above at least one bud. The severed shoots are used for a new crop of cuttings. Poplars are

28. *These shiny metallic chrysomelid beetles are tiny but may be sufficiently numerous to defoliate the tree. They are seen here on grey poplar.*

transplanted out into plantations as rooted cuttings of one to three years old. They may grow 3.7 metres (12 feet) in a single growing season, and they are felled when they are around thirty years old. By this time they will be trees of about 24 metres (80 feet) high and 1.2 metres (4 feet) in girth.

The appeal poplars have for forestry enterprises is understandable as the forester will get a cash return on his investment in thirty to forty-five years. This compares favourably with the forty to eighty years needed for conifers to reach a good market value, and the hundred years or more needed for oaks.

29. *Poplar hawk-moth (Laothoe populi) on Lombardy poplar.*

Poplars for timber, amenity and shelter

Poplar wood is pale, almost white in colour. Unlike other trees, there is little or no deposition of dark-coloured tannins, phenolic compounds or resins in the heartwood, often making it barely discernible from the sapwood. Because these chemicals are absent, the wood is odourless as well as almost colourless and has little natural resistance to fungal attack. This lack of durability and its poor absorption of applied preservatives reduce its value, but nevertheless poplar wood has had a number of uses, past and present. Living poplar trees carry a lot of water, so when first felled the trunk is very full of sap and heavy. In structure the wood is diffuse-porous, that is, the wide water-conducting cells or vessels are scattered evenly throughout the annual growth ring. When it has been seasoned, it is light in weight, with an even straight grain, and soft and easy to use.

Though not a particularly strong wood, it has a tendency to dent rather than splinter when struck, which makes it suitable for certain specialised uses. Traditionally it was used mostly for cart bottoms and floorboards, with sundry other applications including toy manufacture. Black poplar would have been the species used for these purposes in England.

More recently, and still very extensively on the continent of Europe, poplar wood has been used for chip baskets, which are containers for soft fruits, and wooden crates. It is especially useful for packing food, as the absence of any smell prevents it giving a taint. Matches and matchboxes are made from poplar, and an increasing amount is being turned into wood pulp for making various kinds of paper. It is also used very successfully as a component of plywood and particle boards — strong construction materials consisting of chips of wood bonded together with glue. These boards are suitable for interior joinery and furniture making.

Between the 1930s and the 1970s there was a good market in Britain for poplar wood. Many of the new plantations were grown to provide for the match-making and food-container industries. Grants from the Forestry Commission were made available for planting recommended cultivars and trials for breeding new strains were held. Plantations of genetically identical trees were established by taking innumerable cuttings from one promising individual.

The match and chip-basket company Bryant and May Limited was the largest single buyer of British-grown poplar wood and, by providing an almost guaranteed market, encouraged further planting of poplar plantations, but during the 1970s Bryant and May announced that they would no longer require British-produced poplar. The reasons for this were, firstly, that in 1970 the company stopped manufacturing wooden baskets and packaging, as cardboard and plastic products were becoming increasingly cheap to produce, and, secondly, that by 1978 they had decided that they would not be using any more British poplar for match-making, as it was inferior in quality and more expensive than wood grown elsewhere. Since then, the poplar grown in Britain has been used for wood pulp and for the manufacture of plywoods and particle boards, so, despite setbacks, poplar is still a commercially attractive raw material.

Young trees of the selected cultivar can be planted as close together as 2.1 metres (7 feet) to produce straight unbranched poles in a few decades. By coppicing these plantations, the yield can be increased considerably, so that one to three poles are obtained from each stool, cutting on a fifteen-year rotation. The black Italian poplar is also planted as a standard amongst coppiced trees and left to grow into a larger tree felled on a forty- to forty-five-year rotation. This compares favourably with the forty- to eighty-year rotation for fast-growing conifers.

AMENITY

Trees are planted to enhance open spaces and areas where people go for recreation, work or leisure, especially in towns, where it is unlikely that they will be able to establish themselves naturally. Grey, black and black Italian poplars are all trees that lend themselves to amenity planting, in parks, recreation grounds and footpaths beside rivers, where their large spreading crowns may be seen to their best advantage. Lombardy poplars, too, are a very familiar sight in urban and suburban open spaces.

No poplars are suited to the smaller garden, but in larger gardens and estates white and balsam poplars are often planted — the white for its very attractive frosty-white young leaves and shoots and the balsams for the sweet heady scent of the opening buds. The Chinese necklace poplar, perfectly hardy in the south and south-west, is an ornamental and rather curious tree, with its very large red-veined leaves and red petioles, and makes an interesting addition to a garden.

However, poplars planted too close to buildings present a hazard. The fast-growing thirsty roots take up large quantities of water and the removal of this, especially from clay soils, can cause uneven shrinkage below the foundations. This can lead to subsidence, and the majority of cases of damage to buildings by tree roots are caused by poplars.

SHELTER AND SCREENING

The Lombardy poplar is an ideal tree for forming a shelter belt. Because of their narrow unswept crowns, these trees can be planted close together in a row and the young trees grow evenly and fast, quickly making a screen or windbreak. Unlike conifers, Lombardies cast only light shade and the leaf litter does not make the soil beneath acid, but one disadvantage is the short life expectancy. They are often weakened by fungal attack after about thirty years, though individual trees will remain healthy longer.

In the early twentieth century there was widespread planting of railway poplars to screen coal stores, sidings and stations from the view of neighbouring houses. Many maturing hybrid black poplars are in their prime and seen at their best near railways. Fast-growing hybrid black poplars and Lombardies are frequently selected for screening industrial premises — the absence of sucker growth is a further point in their favour and their fresh green foliage and dappled shade in midsummer improve the appearance of otherwise stark factories and offices.

Pests and diseases

INSECT PESTS

Insect pests afflicting poplars are numerous, but only a very few species are restricted to this genus. Most of them will also thrive on willows and sallows, many on other broad-leaved trees. The effects they have on their host vary considerably. When assessing the importance of each pest, the status of the tree is relevant. What may not be of any consequence on wild trees scattered amongst a diversity of other species could be a very serious matter in a nursery or commercial plantation, where a monoculture of many trees is grown in close proximity. As so many species may be found on poplars, only a selection is mentioned here. They include some of those most likely to be devastating on the commercial crop, as well as some noteworthy but uncommon insects.

Aphids such as the woolly poplar aphid (*Phloeomyzus passerini*) and leaf-hoppers such as *Alnetoidea alneti* are two examples of fast-breeding plant bugs (order Hemiptera). The leaf-hopper sucks sap from the leaves, leaving them yellowed. Woolly poplar aphid is one of several aphids that attack poplar, feeding on soft young stems and causing them to wilt and die. As they multiply, colonies of these wax-secreting aphids proliferate in cracks along the branches. They are especially serious in plantations.

Sawflies (order Hymenoptera) that feed on poplars and willows are widely distributed throughout Britain. Four commonly occurring species are the gregarious poplar sawfly (*Nematus melanaspis*), the lesser willow sawfly (*N. pavidus*), the large willow sawfly (*N. salicis*) and the poplar sawfly (*Trichiocampus viminalis*). The greenish larvae of these species either eat away from the leaf surface, leaving a 'skeleton' of veins, or eat in from the leaf edge. There are often two generations a year and, when present in sufficient numbers, they may defoliate the tree completely.

Several species of beetles (order Coleoptera) make their home in poplars. Some feed on the leaves and some, at least one stage of their life cycle, feed in the woody tissues of the trunk and branches. Many of the leaf-eaters belong to the family Chrysomelidae; they include the brassy willow beetle (*Phyllodecta vitellinae*), the blue willow beetle (*P. vulgatissima*) and the large red poplar leaf beetle (*Chrysomela populi*). All these are brightly coloured beetles with a metallic appearance. They are widespread, and both adults and larvae may reduce the leaves of poplars and willows to skeletons.

Of the wood-boring beetles, the large poplar longhorn (*Saperda carcharias*) is one of the most injurious. Found locally throughout Britain, the 30 mm (1¼ inch) long adult selects mature trees on which to lay her eggs. The larvae feed on the more nutritious layer just below the bark and bore an extensive gallery of tunnels. If these galleries ring the main trunk the whole tree dies. The small poplar longhorn (*S. populnea*) is most common in southern England. It attacks younger wood, preferring aspens.

Another wood-boring beetle with a chiefly southerly distribution is the osier weevil (*Cryptorhynchus lapathi*). Though more usually attacking willows and alder, when it turns its attentions to poplar plantations and nurseries the larvae can wreak havoc by boring galleries through twigs, branches and trunks of both young and old trees. The quality of the wood is impaired, and the tree weakened or killed.

The larvae of the large tortoiseshell butterfly (*Nymphalis polychloros*) feed on poplar leaves. This now rare insect is found very infrequently in a few localities in south-east England and is not classed as a pest. Neither are two other members of the order Lepidoptera, the poplar and eyed hawk-moths (*Laothoe populi* and *Smerinthus ocellata*), whose larvae also eat poplar foliage.

A number of moths, however, are poplar pests. Many members of the prominent family (Notodontidae) feed on the foliage, including the puss-moth (*Cerura vinula*) and the pebble prominent (*Eligmodonta ziczac*). The larvae of both are curiously shaped, with conspicuous protuberances. The puss-moth caterpillar is particularly bizarre, revealing when threatened two black false 'eyes' and a forked tail with two lashing red filaments. They may cause serious damage in plantations.

A rather less endearing moth, the goat moth (*Cossus cossus*), has larvae that burrow deep into the tree trunk. Here they live for three to four years, by which time the yellow and pinkish larva is about 75 mm (3 inches) long. They are renowned for their foul goat-like smell and for the damage they do to many broad-leaved trees, including fruit trees and poplars. Older trees are favoured and it was formerly a nuisance in orchards. Although it may still infest more mature plantations, it is much less common than it once was and is more likely to afflict individual poplars growing in parks and gardens. Adult goat moths are a pale mottled brown, the larger females having a wingspan of 90 mm (3½ inches).

Another species with wood-boring larvae is the attractive leopard moth (*Zeuzera pyrina*), found mostly in southern England. Adults are white with black spots. The caterpillars tunnel along beneath the bark for two to three years, causing weakened branchlets to snap off. The hornet moth (*Sesia apiformis*) is a locally distributed species most likely to be seen in East Anglia. In spite of their unnerving resemblance to hornets, the adults are harmless, but their larvae feed by burrowing into the roots and lower trunk of poplars and sallows.

One of the most serious poplar pests, especially of trees grown for timber, is the poplar cambium midge (*Agromyza* species). Widespread and often very numerous, these tiny flies produce larvae that burrow along stem cambium. Though only 1 mm (0.04 inches) wide, each larva grows to 15 to 30 mm (0.6 to 1.2 inches) long and the damage they do to the commercial value of the timber is considerable. A heavy attack will kill the tree. Both this midge and the less harmful poplar gall midge (*Contarinia petioli*) belong to the order Diptera. The gall midge usually chooses aspen as a host plant, and the tiny larvae attack the leaves, inducing a small pinkish gall.

BACTERIAL AND FUNGAL DISEASES

The disease known as bacterial canker is the biggest scourge of poplar plantations. Caused by the bacterium *Xanthomonas populi,* it afflicts particularly the black poplars, the balsam poplars and the hybrids of black and balsam poplars. It hampers poplar cultivation in Britain and other north-west European countries. Black, white and grey poplars are resistant to this disease and the black hybrids inherit their predisposition to it from the North American cottonwood. One of the chief aims of poplar research is the development of cultivars resistant to this canker.

The bacteria enter the tree through the bud scales and stipule traces in spring. The infection is seen as a weeping bacterial slime usually at the bases of buds on young shoots. This causes die-back of the infected shoots, and the disease spreads through susceptible trees, with oozing patches of canker appearing on branches and trunk. There is no cure, and affected trees are burnt to prevent the bacterial exudate from being carried to other trees by insects and birds.

Various fungi cause diseases of leaves, trunks and branches, or roots, but in Britain none is as serious as bacterial canker. Probably the most commonly encountered is rust, caused by a number of species of *Melampsora,* many of which are widespread throughout Britain. These fungi attack poplar leaves, producing bright orange spots on the lower surface and blackish ones on the upper. To complete its life cycle, the fungus needs a second host — sometimes another tree, such as larch or Scots pine, and sometimes a herbaceous plant such as dog's mercury and species of *Allium.* A heavy infection may impair the growth rate but does not kill the tree.

Plantation trees are felled whilst too young for attacks by wood-rotting fungi, but trees over sixty years old are often infected by bracket fungi such as *Ganoderma applanatum, Fomes* species and *Polyporus* species. The honey fungus (*Armillaria mellea*) will occasionally attack poplar roots. Poplar is also one of the trees favoured by the parasitic flowering plant mistletoe (*Viscum album*).

Further reading

Bevan, D. *Forest Insects.* Forestry Commission Handbook number 1, 1987.

Clapham, A. R.; Tutin, T. G.; and Warburg, E. F. *Flora of the British Isles.* Cambridge University Press, 1962.

Food and Agriculture Organisation of the United Nations. *Poplars and Willows in Wood Production and Land Use.* FAO Forestry Series number 10, 1979.

Meikle, R. D. *Willows and Poplars of Great Britain and Ireland.* BSBI Handbook number 4, 1984.

Mitchell, A. *A Field Guide to the Trees of Britain and Northern Europe.* Collins, 1974.

Phillips, R. *Trees in Britain, Europe and North America.* Pan, 1978.

ACKNOWLEDGEMENTS

The author wishes to thank E. H. Herbert for the use of photographs on the front cover and in figures 4, 14, 21 and 23. All the other illustrations are by the author.